A sturdy start to SPaG from CGP!

These Foundation 10-Minute Tests are spot-on for pupils who are finding KS2 grammar, punctuation and spelling tough. They're packed with simple questions to help them build the basic skills they'll need for the SATs.

Answers to every question are at the back of the book, along with a handy progress chart to keep track of their marks.

We've even included pull-out scripts for each spelling test, with the full audio files downloadable from:

www.cgpbooks.co.uk/KS210MinTests

What CGP is all about

Our sole aim here at CGP is to produce the highest quality books — carefully written, immaculately presented and dangerously close to being funny.

Then we work our socks off to get them out to you — at the cheapest possible prices.

Contents

Set A

Grammar & Punctuation Test 1 2
Grammar & Punctuation Test 2 6
Grammar & Punctuation Test 3 10
Grammar & Punctuation Test 4 14
Spelling Test 18
Puzzle 19
Scoresheet 20

Set B

Grammar & Punctuation Test 1 21
Grammar & Punctuation Test 2 25
Grammar & Punctuation Test 3 29
Grammar & Punctuation Test 4 33
Spelling Test 37
Puzzle 38
Scoresheet 39

Set C

Grammar & Punctuation Test 1 40
Grammar & Punctuation Test 2 44
Grammar & Punctuation Test 3 48
Grammar & Punctuation Test 4 52
Spelling Test 56
Puzzle 57
Scoresheet 58

Hints and Tips 59
Answers 60
Progress Chart 70

The transcripts for the spelling tests can be found in a pull-out section in the middle of the book, or you can use the online audio files.

Published by CGP

Editors: Andy Cashmore, Catherine Heygate, Melissa Gardner, Hannah Roscoe
With thanks to Juliette Green and Holly Robinson for the proofreading.

ISBN: 978 1 78908 445 0
Clipart from Corel®
Printed by Elanders Ltd, Newcastle upon Tyne.
Based on the classic CGP style created by Richard Parsons.

Text, design, layout and original illustrations © Coordination Group Publications Ltd. (CGP) 2019
All rights reserved.

Photocopying this book is not permitted, even if you have a CLA licence.
Extra copies are available from CGP with next day delivery • 0800 1712 712 • www.cgpbooks.co.uk

Set A: Grammar & Punctuation 1

There are **12 questions** in this test. Give yourself **10 minutes** to answer them all.

1. Tick the sentence that is an **exclamation**.

   tick **one** box

   I just saw a great show ☐

   What was that show about ☐

   What a tremendous show that was ☐

   Go and see this show ☐

   1 mark

2. The sentence below is missing a **comma**.
   Tick **one** box to show where the comma should go.

   We saw a bridge a skyscraper and a stadium.

   1 mark

3. Circle the **adjective** in each of the sentences below.

   Adjectives are words that describe nouns.

   Michael danced in the local competition.

   I'm furious that Billy barely tried to help us.

   1 mark

4. Circle the **subordinating conjunction** in the sentence below.

   A conjunction is a word that joins two clauses.

   I put up the tent while Anika collected wood.

   1 mark

5. Circle the **possessive pronoun** in each of the sentences below.

   Natalie said the green bike was hers.

   The paint is ours because we paid for it.

   I thought the magazine was mine.

   1 mark

6. Draw a line to match each word to a **suffix** to make a new word. The first one has been done for you.

   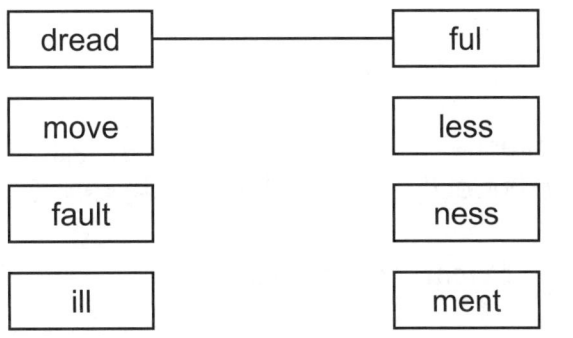

   Only use each suffix once.

   1 mark

7. Tick the sentence that uses a **preposition**.

tick **one** box

The white car was slow. ☐

I dislike carrots and broccoli. ☐

Sarah put the cake tin on the table. ☐

We all whispered quietly. ☐

Prepositions can tell you where things are.

1 mark

8. Underline the **relative clause** in the sentence below.

They went into the cave, where it was very gloomy.

1 mark

9. Read the sentence below. Circle the correct form of the verb in brackets to complete the sentence in the **present perfect** form.

Louise (wrote / has written) a short story.

1 mark

10. Add a **semi-colon** to the sentence below so that it's punctuated correctly.

A semi-colon can join two main clauses.

The museum was boring I went to the cinema.

1 mark

11. Tick the sentence that uses the **present progressive** form.

tick **one** box

We danced to the music. ☐

Gina is closing the curtains. ☐

Maria was waiting for you. ☐

The present progressive form shows something happening right now.

1 mark

12. Rewrite the sentence below using the correct punctuation for **direct speech**.

Direct speech starts with a capital letter.

He said the shop is closed.

....

....

1 mark

END OF TEST

/12

Set A: Grammar & Punctuation 2

There are **11 questions** in this test. Give yourself **10 minutes** to answer them all.

1. The sentence below is missing two **capital letters**.
   Tick **two** boxes to show which words need a capital letter.

   They asked me to visit, but i can't go to germany this year.

   1 mark

2. Look at the table below. Put a tick in each row to show which **punctuation mark** should be used at the end of each sentence.

Sentence	Full stop	Question mark
Tamara will be back soon		
When does the plane arrive		
This isn't Kyle's house		

   1 mark

3. Underline the longest **noun phrase** in the sentence below.

   I drew on the shiny whiteboard yesterday.

   1 mark

4. Read the sentences below. Tick the **two** sentences that use the **simple past** tense.

                                                                                            tick **two** boxes

The swimmer dives into the pool.	☐
We will find a way to solve this problem.	☐
The skater skidded around the corner.	☐
Giselle trekked up the tallest mountain.	☐

1 mark

5. Draw a line to match each sentence to the **type of sentence** it is.

Find your backpack now	statement
There's butter in the fridge	question
Which way is the hospital	command

1 mark

6. Read the sentences below. Replace the words that are underlined with the correct **pronoun**.

Lee couldn't find the key, so <u>Lee</u> was locked out.

Jay and Max had a nap, but <u>Jay and Max</u> were still tired.

1 mark

7. Read the sentence below. Tick **one** box to show which word is missing an **apostrophe**.

The twins rode their bikes to Sams house to see his new gerbils.

1 mark

8. Put a letter in each box to show the **subject** and the **object** in the sentence below.

subject A   object B

The customers ate the soup.

1 mark

9. Draw a line to match each word to the correct **synonym**.

cheerful   keen

honest   jolly

eager   truthful

annoy   irritate

A synonym is a word that has the same, or nearly the same, meaning as another word.

1 mark

10. Add a **dash** to the sentence below so that it's punctuated correctly.

   I really like cats I draw pictures of them all the time.

   1 mark

11. Write your own sentence using the word <u>wash</u> as a **verb**. Use correct punctuation in your sentence. Do not change the word <u>wash</u>.

   A verb is a doing or being word.

   ....

   ....

   Write your own sentence using the word <u>wash</u> as a **noun**. Use correct punctuation in your sentence. Do not change the word <u>wash</u>.

   A noun is a word that names something.

   ....

   ....

   2 marks

END OF TEST

/12

Set A: Grammar & Punctuation 3

There are **12 questions** in this test. Give yourself **10 minutes** to answer them all.

1. Circle the **two nouns** in the sentence below.

   The talented teenager played his flute perfectly.

   1 mark

2. Add a **comma** to the sentence below so that it's punctuated correctly.

   Tomorrow evening I am going to my piano lesson.

   1 mark

3. Read the sentence below.
   Tick the sentence that should come **after** it.

   We went to the zoo yesterday afternoon.

   tick **one** box

   We saw some monkeys and a zebra. ☐
   We seen some monkeys and a zebra. ☐
   We will see some monkeys and a zebra. ☐
   We are seeing some monkeys and a zebra. ☐

   1 mark

4. The sentence below is missing two **brackets**.
   Tick **two** boxes to show where the brackets should go.

   The goldfish ↑ my first pet ↑ is ↑ a year old today.
   ☐   ☐   ☐   ☐

   Brackets go around extra information in a sentence.

   1 mark

5. Read the sentences below. Choose a **conjunction** from the box to fill each gap and write it on the line.

> or   so   and

Only use each conjunction once.

Nisha thought it would be sunny, ... she brought a hat .... a bottle of water. However, she didn't bring her sunglasses .... a picnic for lunch.

1 mark

6. Draw a line to match each sentence to the correct **determiner**.

Olivia saw .... goat.	a
They haven't got .... time.	an
Can I buy .... electric toothbrush?	much

1 mark

7. Complete the table by turning the adjectives into **adverbs**. The first one has been done for you.

Adjective	Adverb
quick	quickly
furious	
sloppy	

You might need to change the spelling of the adjective when you turn it into an adverb.

1 mark

8. Circle the **modal verb** in the sentence below.

   It might snow later today.

   Modal verbs can show how likely something is.

   1 mark

9. Tick the sentence that uses a **hyphen** correctly.

   tick **one** box

   Tristan often swims in the cold-sea. ☐

   The pet-friendly hotel was excellent. ☐

   Painting-quickly made the picture look messy. ☐

   1 mark

10. Underline the **relative pronoun** in each of the sentences below.

    I met a girl who was from Australia.

    Let's find a clover that has four leaves.

    The chicken, which lives in the barn, is very noisy.

    A relative pronoun is just one word.

    1 mark

11. Rewrite the list below in **bullet point** form.
    Remember to punctuate your answer correctly.

    Akira is going to finish his history homework, play baseball and read a book.

    Akira is going to do these things:

    • ....

    • ....

    • ....

    1 mark

12. Look at the **word family** below.
    What does the root <u>ped</u> mean?

    Think about what each word means and how their meanings might be linked.

    pedal   millipede   pedestrian

    tick **one** box

    stop   ☐

    foot   ☐

    insect ☐

    1 mark

END OF TEST

/12

Set A: Grammar & Punctuation 4

There are **12 questions** in this test. Give yourself **10 minutes** to answer them all.

1. Circle the word in the sentence below that needs an **apostrophe**.

   The guards wouldnt let the reporters into the bank.

   1 mark

2. Draw a line to match each sentence to the correct **punctuation mark**. Use each punctuation mark once.

What a strange quiz that was	.
I think they've gone home	?
Why didn't anyone tell me	!

   1 mark

3. Circle the **conjunction** in each of the sentences below.

   My baby sister cried because she was hungry.

   Tyler always grumbles when he cleans his room.

   1 mark

Set A: Grammar & Punctuation 4

4. Read the sentence below.
   What is '**We stayed at the beach**' an example of?

   We stayed at the beach until it got dark.

	tick **one** box
a subordinate clause	☐
a main clause	☐
a preposition	☐
an adverbial	☐

   1 mark

5. Tick the sentence that is a **command**.

	tick **one** box
She demanded to know what had happened.	☐
Get down before they see you.	☐
How could we have been spotted?	☐

   1 mark

6. Underline the **adverbial** in the sentence below.

   The fairground ride was over very quickly.

   An adverbial is a word or group of words that acts like an adverb.

   1 mark

7. Put a tick in each row to show whether each sentence is **formal** or **informal**.

Sentence	Formal	Informal
The house is freezing, don't you think?		
We are delighted to accept this award.		
It is vital that he attend.		

1 mark

8. Draw a line to match each **prefix** with the correct root word. The first one has been done for you.

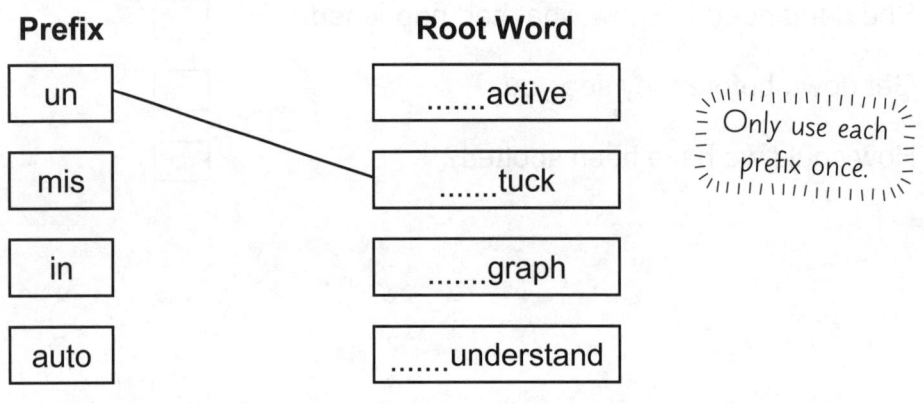

Only use each prefix once.

1 mark

9. Add a **colon** to the sentence below so that it's punctuated correctly.

A colon can introduce an explanation.

We were happy Dad said we could go to the park.

1 mark

10. Tick the sentence that contains a **relative clause**.

tick **one** box

The football course will last four weeks. ☐

Grace, who is good at art, will draw a picture. ☐

Charlie couldn't believe what she saw. ☐

1 mark

11. Read the two sentences below. Explain how the **comma** changes the meaning of the second sentence.

Harry buys chocolate cake and apples.

Harry buys chocolate, cake and apples.

....

....

....

1 mark

12. Tick the sentence that is written in the **active** voice.

In an active sentence, the subject does something.

tick **one** box

The blackbird was chased by a quick cat. ☐

James was thanked by the old man. ☐

The bulldozer destroyed the mansion. ☐

1 mark

END OF TEST

/12

Set A: Spelling Test

For this test, you'll need someone to **read out** the transcript from the middle of the book, or you can use the **online audio file**. The test will take about 10 minutes.

mark box

1. Tammy played .... with her toys. ☐

2. He is .... good at hockey. ☐

3. We got a train from the .... ☐

4. I did some .... for my history project. ☐

5. We are going to get into .... for this. ☐

6. Kevin made a .... cake for Harriet's birthday. ☐

7. I could hear the .... of our footsteps. ☐

8. Jenny will .... before everyone else. ☐

9. Everyone was very .... during the school trip. ☐

10. There were lots of .... in the classroom. ☐

11. Dev wanted to .... to France. ☐

12. The identity of the jewel thief was a .... ☐

/12

Set A: Puzzle

This puzzle is a great way to practise your suffix skills.

Parrot Pandemonium

Four pirates have lost their parrots, and you need to reunite them. Each parrot is carrying a root word and each pirate has a suffix on their flag. Match the parrots and the pirates by drawing a line between each root word and the suffix that can be added to it. Then write the completed word beside the correct pirate. Be careful — some of the root words may change their spelling when the suffix is added!

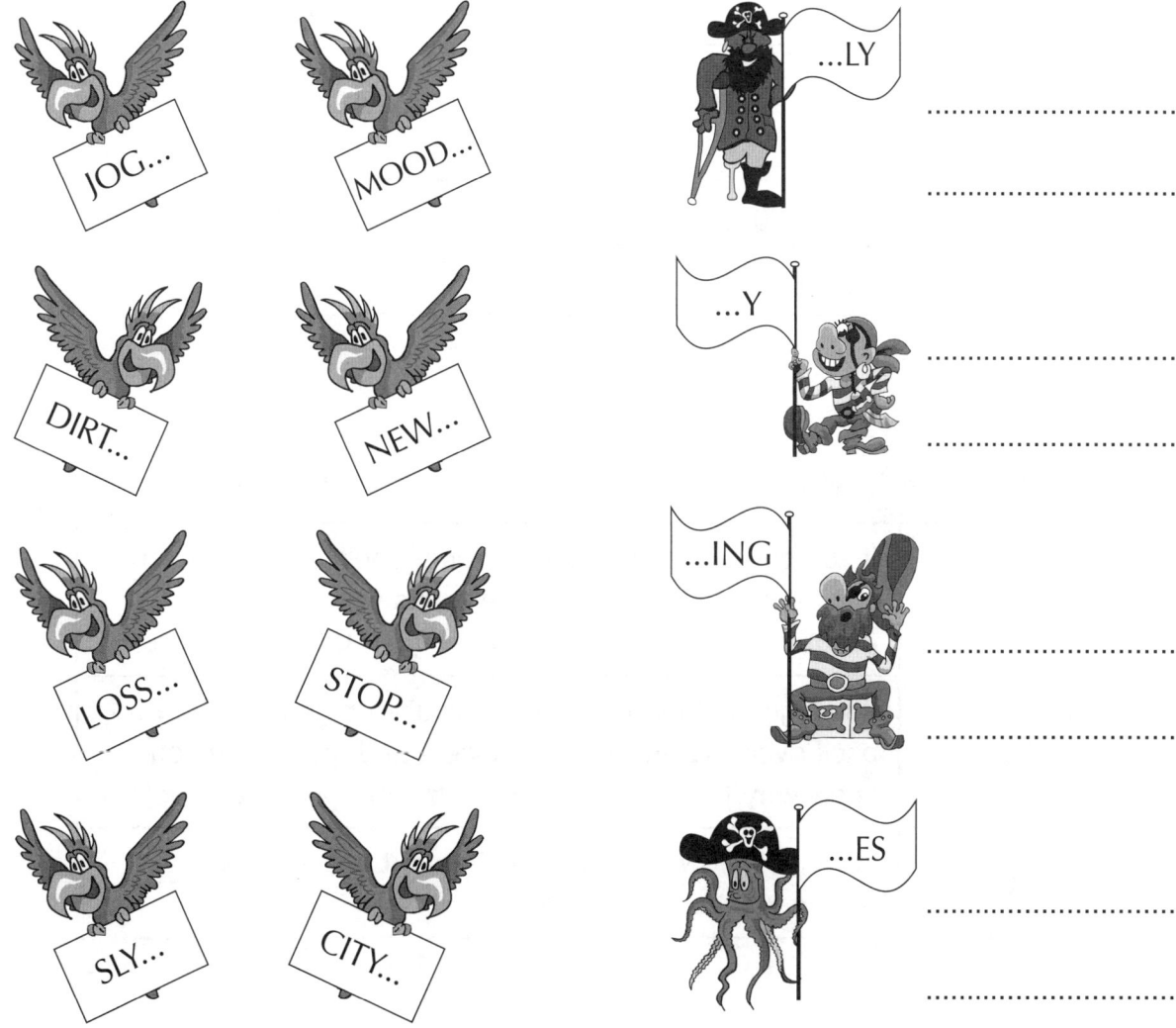

End of Set A: Scoresheet

You've finished a full set of tests — well done!

Now it's time to put your scores in here
and see how you're getting on.

	Score	
Test 1		/12
Test 2		/12
Test 3		/12
Test 4		/12
Spelling Test		/12
Total		**/60**

Once you've got a score out of 60, check it out in the table below...

0 – 29	If you got a lot of questions wrong, don't worry. Ask an adult to help you work out the **areas** you need **more practice** on. Then have another go at **this** set of tests.
30 – 45	If you got half-marks or better, you're doing well. **Read** back over your **incorrect** answers and make sure you know **why** they're wrong. Then try the **next set** of tests.
46 – 60	Woohoo! Now have a go at the **next set** of tests — can you beat your score?

Set B: Grammar & Punctuation 1

There are **12 questions** in this test. Give yourself **10 minutes** to answer them all.

1. Circle the **verb** in the sentence below.

   The kangaroo bounced towards the meadow.

   1 mark

2. Read the sentence below. Circle the correct form of the verb in brackets to complete the sentence in the **present tense**.

   Ellen (rows / rowed / will row) her boat down the river.

   1 mark

3. Tick the **two** sentences that are **statements**.

	tick **two** boxes
Would you like a piece of toast	☐
What an incredible journey that was	☐
Abha's pebble was smoother than mine	☐
I might do my homework on the bus	☐

   1 mark

4. Underline the **co-ordinating conjunction** in the sentence below.

   I left my wallet at home, so Abbey paid for dinner.

   1 mark

5. The sentence below is missing a **comma**.
Tick **one** box to show where the comma should go.

Early each morning Pascal goes for a jog.
☐   ☐ ☐ ☐

1 mark

6. Read the sentence below.
What is '**My easily startled auntie**' an example of?

My easily startled auntie was terrified of the popping balloons.

tick **one** box

a subordinate clause ☐

an adverbial ☐

a noun phrase ☐

1 mark

7. Rewrite the list below in **bullet point** form.
Remember to punctuate your answer correctly.

The shop sells camping equipment, hiking boots and sunglasses.

The shop sells these items:

- ....
- ....
- ....

1 mark

8. Put a letter in each box to show which **word class** the underlined words belong to.

| adjective | determiner | adverb |
| A | B | C |

My <u>brave</u> sister <u>fearlessly</u> took <u>the</u> spider outside.

☐   ☐   ☐

1 mark

9. Tick the **two** sentences that use **colons** correctly.

tick **two** boxes

I dislike three things: moths, wasps and bees. ☐

They wore blue jumpers: they also wore black shorts. ☐

Hachiro was upset: he'd lost his backpack. ☐

The garden has roses: daffodils: and tulips. ☐

1 mark

10. Add **two dashes** to the sentence below so that it's punctuated correctly.

If you remove the words between the dashes, the sentence should still make sense.

My ball which I got on holiday is stuck in a tree.

1 mark

11. Complete the table below by writing a suitable **antonym** of each word. The first one has been done for you.

Word	Antonym
wet	dry
sleepy	
boring	

An antonym is a word that means the opposite of another word.

1 mark

12. Tick the sentence that uses the **subjunctive**.

The subjunctive can be used in sentences about situations that aren't real.

tick **one** box

I used my blocks to build a castle. ☐

If I were a bear, I would eat nothing but honey. ☐

We are going on a school trip tomorrow. ☐

1 mark

END OF TEST

/12

Set B: Grammar & Punctuation 2

There are **12 questions** in this test. Give yourself **10 minutes** to answer them all.

1. Tick the word that always needs a **capital letter**.

   tick **one** box

   flamingo ☐

   friend ☐

   saturday ☐

   life ☐

   1 mark

2. Tick **two** boxes to show the **pronouns** in the sentence below.

   She found a rare coin and hid it in the wardrobe.
   ↑   ↑   ↑   ↑
   ☐   ☐   ☐   ☐

   1 mark

3. Rewrite the sentence below as a **command**.

   Could you take Ryan to his doctor's appointment?

   ....

   ....

   1 mark

4. Tick the **prefix** below that could be added to all of these words.

   star   visor   hero

   tick **one** box

   anti-   ☐
   mega-   ☐
   super- ☐
   ad-   ☐

   1 mark

5. Read the sentence below.
   Circle the most suitable **pronoun** to complete the sentence.

   It was their trophy, but now it is ....

   we   us   ours   our

   1 mark

6. Add a **comma** to the sentence below to show that Alex is asking Leigh whether they should leave.

   Do you think we should leave Leigh?

   1 mark

7. Tick the sentence that uses the **past progressive** form.

	tick **one** box
The cat was sitting outside.	☐
Preena darts across the playground.	☐
The window is cracked.	☐
Our bus will definitely be late.	☐

The past progressive is a type of past tense.

1 mark

8. Tick the sentence that contains a **preposition**.

	tick **one** box
Sophie made her way slowly through the tunnel.	☐
I swept the floor while you cleaned the sink.	☐
You can have an apple or a kiwi.	☐

1 mark

9. Read the sentence below. Add **two semi-colons** so that it's punctuated correctly.

Semi-colons can be used to separate lists of longer things.

On my pizza, I normally have tomatoes, but not too many a few mushrooms and plenty of cheese.

1 mark

10. Underline the **subordinate clause** in the sentence below.

    Claude won the trophy because he beat Florence.

    1 mark

11. The sentence below is missing a **hyphen**.
    Tick **one** box to show where the hyphen should go.

    A well □ known □ author visited our □ school last □ week.

    1 mark

12. Put a tick in each row to show whether each sentence is written in the **passive** voice or the **active** voice. The first one has been done for you.

Sentence	Passive	Active
The swan landed in the pond.		✓
Ben sings into the microphone.		
The lamp was knocked over by the child.		

    In a passive sentence, something is done to the subject.

    1 mark

END OF TEST

/12

Set B: Grammar & Punctuation 3

There are **12 questions** in this test. Give yourself **10 minutes** to answer them all.

1. Read the sentence below.
   Which **word class** does the word '**milkman**' belong to?

   The local **milkman** always whistles while he's driving.

   tick **one** box

   noun ☐

   verb ☐

   adjective ☐

   pronoun ☐

   1 mark

2. Add a **comma** to the sentence below so that it's punctuated correctly.

   The zoo had giant pandas zebras and elephants.

   1 mark

3. The sentence below is missing two sets of **inverted commas**. Tick **two** boxes to show where the inverted commas should go.

   Inverted commas are also called speech marks.

   Mrs Harrison is coming over later , said Joey.
   ↑   ↑   ↑   ↑
   ☐   ☐   ☐   ☐

   1 mark

4. Circle the correct word in brackets to complete each sentence using **Standard English**.

We (isn't / aren't) doing our homework tonight.

I don't want (nothing / anything) on my toast.

1 mark

5. Read the sentence below. Change all the underlined verbs from the **simple present** tense to the **simple past** tense.

The footballer <u>runs</u> across the pitch and <u>passes</u> the ball.

1 mark

6. Tick the sentence that uses the **present perfect** form.

	tick **one** box
Lin goes on the roller-coaster.	☐
She has lived in Canada for years.	☐
We went to the new restaurant in town.	☐

The present perfect uses the simple present tense of 'have'.

1 mark

7. Underline the **relative pronoun** in the sentence below.

   John, <u>whose</u> birthday it was, missed his own party.

   1 mark

8. Rewrite the sentence below with the **adverbial** at the beginning. Make sure you use the same words and the correct punctuation.

   Nadeema goes for long bike rides on Sundays.

   ....

   ....

   1 mark

9. Put a tick in each row of the table to show whether the words in bold are a **main clause** or a **subordinate clause**.

Sentence	Main clause	Subordinate clause
Jess uses Bruce's room when he is away.		
After the river flooded, the road was closed.		
I cleaned my boots **before I came inside**.		

   Main clauses make sense on their own, but subordinate clauses don't.

   1 mark

10. The sentence below is missing a **dash**.
Tick **one** box to show where the dash should go.

I ate fried squid ☐ for the first ☐ time ☐ it was delicious.

1 mark

11. Underline the **object** in the sentence below.

The parrot held the cracker.

1 mark

12. Look at the word in the box below.
Tick the word that is **not** in the same **word family**.

press

tick **one** box
pressure ☐
express ☐
squeeze ☐
impressed ☐

1 mark

END OF TEST

/12

Set B: Grammar & Punctuation 4

There are **12 questions** in this test. Give yourself **10 minutes** to answer them all.

1. Read the sentence below. What **type of sentence** is it?

   What a nightmare this train journey is!

   tick **one** box
   - statement ☐
   - question ☐
   - command ☐
   - exclamation ☐

   1 mark

2. Underline the correct **conjunction** in brackets to complete the sentence below.

   Marlene listens to pop music all the time,

   (nor / but / or) she never listens to country music.

   1 mark

3. Add a **question mark** or an **exclamation mark** at the end of each sentence below so that they are punctuated correctly.

   How disgusting that was ...

   How did the thief get into the safe ...

   1 mark

4. Underline the **possessive pronoun** in each of the sentences below.

   We discovered that the statue was theirs.

   I forgot to bring a coat, so Gareth lent me his.

   1 mark

5. Write a sensible **question** to fit the answer below.

   I arrived at the campsite on Friday evening.

   ....

   ....

   1 mark

6. Read the sentence below.
   What is '**Alf decided to build a snowman**' an example of?

   While it was snowing outside, **Alf decided to build a snowman**.

   tick **one** box

   a subordinate clause ☐

   a main clause ☐

   a preposition ☐

   an adverbial ☐

   1 mark

Key Stage 2
10-Minute Tests
Spelling Test Transcripts

The spelling tests need to be **read out loud** to the children.

You can read the tests out loud to the children by following the instructions below, or you can play an **audio file** from here: www.cgpbooks.co.uk/ks210mintests

---

Each test should take about 10 minutes.

For each test, read out the following instructions, and then answer any questions the children have.

- Listen to the instructions I'm about to give you.
- I'm going to read out twelve sentences. These sentences are printed on your answer page, but each one has a word missing. Listen to the missing word and write it in. Make sure you spell it correctly.
- I will read the word, then read the word within a sentence, then I'll say the word a third time.
- The test will now begin.

Now read the spellings to the children:

- Say the spelling number.
- Say "The word is..."
- Read out the word in its sentence.
- Say "The word is..."
- Pause for at least 12 seconds between each of the spellings.

At the end of each test, read out all 12 sentences again, and give the children time to change their answers if they want to.

When the test is over, say "This is the end of the test."

© CGP — not to be photocopied

Set A: Spelling Questions

> Read out the instructions from the **first page** of this pull-out. Then read out the following:

1. Spelling one.
   The word is **happily**.
   *Tammy played **happily** with her toys.*
   The word is **happily**.

2. Spelling two.
   The word is **quite**.
   *He is **quite** good at hockey.*
   The word is **quite**.

3. Spelling three.
   The word is **station**.
   *We got a train from the **station**.*
   The word is **station**.

4. Spelling four.
   The word is **research**.
   *I did some **research** for my history project.*
   The word is **research**.

5. Spelling five.
   The word is **trouble**.
   *We are going to get into **trouble** for this.*
   The word is **trouble**.

6. Spelling six.
   The word is **special**.
   *Kevin made a **special** cake for Harriet's birthday.*
   The word is **special**.

7. Spelling seven.
   The word is **echo**.
   *I could hear the **echo** of our footsteps.*
   The word is **echo**.

8. Spelling eight.
   The word is **arrive**.
   *Jenny will **arrive** before everyone else.*
   The word is **arrive**.

9. Spelling nine.
   The word is **sensible**.
   *Everyone was very **sensible** during the school trip.*
   The word is **sensible**.

10. Spelling ten.
    The word is **flies**.
    *There were lots of **flies** in the classroom.*
    The word is **flies**.

11. Spelling eleven.
    The word is **travel**.
    *Dev wanted to **travel** to France.*
    The word is **travel**.

12. Spelling twelve.
    The word is **mystery**.
    *The identity of the jewel thief was a **mystery**.*
    The word is **mystery**.

> At the end of the test, read out **all 12** sentences again, and give the children time to change their answers if they want to.
> When the test is over, say "This is the end of the test."

© CGP — not to be photocopied

Set B: Spelling Questions

> Read out the instructions from the **first page** of this pull-out. Then read out the following:

1. Spelling one.
   The word is **paper**.
   *She drew a map on a piece of **paper**.*
   The word is **paper**.

2. Spelling two.
   The word is **worth**.
   *The ring was **worth** a lot of money.*
   The word is **worth**.

3. Spelling three.
   The word is **young**.
   *My sister is too **young** to go to school.*
   The word is **young**.

4. Spelling four.
   The word is **nicest**.
   *My dad is the **nicest** person I know.*
   The word is **nicest**.

5. Spelling five.
   The word is **science**.
   *Their final **science** experiment was a success.*
   The word is **science**.

6. Spelling six.
   The word is **eight**.
   *There are **eight** bowls on the table.*
   The word is **eight**.

7. Spelling seven.
   The word is **rough**.
   *The stone felt very **rough**.*
   The word is **rough**.

8. Spelling eight.
   The word is **position**.
   *Martin was sitting in an uncomfortable **position**.*
   The word is **position**.

9. Spelling nine.
   The word is **gardener**.
   *The school **gardener** mowed the playing field.*
   The word is **gardener**.

10. Spelling ten.
    The word is **notice**.
    *Emily didn't **notice** the new wallpaper.*
    The word is **notice**.

11. Spelling eleven.
    The word is **illegal**.
    *It is **illegal** to steal money from a bank.*
    The word is **illegal**.

12. Spelling twelve.
    The word is **ceiling**.
    *Ravi hit his head on the **ceiling**.*
    The word is **ceiling**.

> At the end of the test, read out **all 12** sentences again, and give the children time to change their answers if they want to.
> When the test is over, say "This is the end of the test."

© CGP — not to be photocopied

Set C: Spelling Questions

> Read out the instructions from the **first page** of this pull-out. Then read out the following:

1. Spelling one.
   The word is **group**.
   A **group** of girls entered the post office.
   The word is **group**.

2. Spelling two.
   The word is **build**.
   We wanted to **build** a treehouse.
   The word is **build**.

3. Spelling three.
   The word is **earth**.
   The **earth** was wet after the rain.
   The word is **earth**.

4. Spelling four.
   The word is **finally**.
   The artist had **finally** finished their painting.
   The word is **finally**.

5. Spelling five.
   The word is **picture**.
   Clara took a **picture** of the woman in the hat.
   The word is **picture**.

6. Spelling six.
   The word is **entrance**.
   The **entrance** to the shop was blocked.
   The word is **entrance**.

7. Spelling seven.
   The word is **bought**.
   Romina **bought** Carey a new umbrella.
   The word is **bought**.

8. Spelling eight.
   The word is **serious**.
   The teacher's expression was very **serious**.
   The word is **serious**.

9. Spelling nine.
   The word is **enjoyable**.
   It has been an **enjoyable** day out.
   The word is **enjoyable**.

10. Spelling ten.
    The word is **referee**.
    The players were polite to the **referee**.
    The word is **referee**.

11. Spelling eleven.
    The word is **tongue**.
    I burnt my **tongue** on my hot chocolate.
    The word is **tongue**.

12. Spelling twelve.
    The word is **student**.
    The **student** did all of his homework on time.
    The word is **student**.

> At the end of the test, read out **all 12** sentences again, and give the children time to change their answers if they want to.
> When the test is over, say "This is the end of the test."

7. The sentence below is missing a **colon**.
   Tick **one** box to show where the colon should go.

   You'll need these things ↑ for school ↑ a jumper, a bag, □ □

   a pencil case ↑ and a new set of pens. □

   1 mark

8. Circle the **adverb** in the sentence below.

   She will probably meet us at the supermarket.

   1 mark

9. Read the words below.
   Tick the word which is an **adjective** made by adding a suffix to the word 'hope'.

	tick **one** box
hoped	□
hopeless	□
hopefully	□

   Remember, adjectives are words that describe nouns.

   1 mark

10. Underline the **relative clause** in the sentence below.

    We hid in the cupboard, which was very cramped.

    1 mark

11. Tick **one** box to show the **modal verb** in the sentence below.

We should invite our friends over at the weekend.
  ↑   ↑   ↑   ↑
  ☐   ☐   ☐   ☐

1 mark

12. Read the two sentences below. Explain how the position of the **apostrophe** gives the two sentences different meanings.

These are the girl's shoes.

These are the girls' shoes.

....

....

....

1 mark

END OF TEST

/12

Set B: Spelling Test

For this test, you'll need someone to **read out** the transcript from the middle of the book, or you can use the **online audio file**. The test will take about 10 minutes.

mark box

1. She drew a map on a piece of ....

2. The ring was .... a lot of money.

3. My sister is too .... to go to school.

4. My dad is the .... person I know.

5. Their final .... experiment was a success.

6. There are .... bowls on the table.

7. The stone felt very ....

8. Martin was sitting in an uncomfortable ....

9. The school .... mowed the playing field.

10. Emily didn't .... the new wallpaper.

11. It is .... to steal money from a bank.

12. Ravi hit his head on the ....

/12

Set B: Puzzle

This puzzle is a brilliant way to practise your punctuation skills.

Aliens and Apostrophes

Zorga the alien has forgotten the code to unlock her spaceship. All the sentences below have numbers in them. Underline the numbers in all the sentences that use apostrophes correctly. Write them in the boxes at the bottom to give Zorga the code to get into her spaceship.

Sally went to the cinema with two of her brother's.

Some people believe that cats have nine lives, but I do'nt think so.

Ms Wright's Year Eight class was the biggest in the school.

That's the last time I'm telling you three anything!

One day, I'll be famous and youll be sorry.

Noam and his friends' ate ten cakes between them.

James's uncle gave him a five pound note.

My mum says that sevens her lucky number.

I called Zuri's number six times, but she didn't answer.

We're going to sing four songs at Erika's wedding.

The code to unlock the spaceship is:

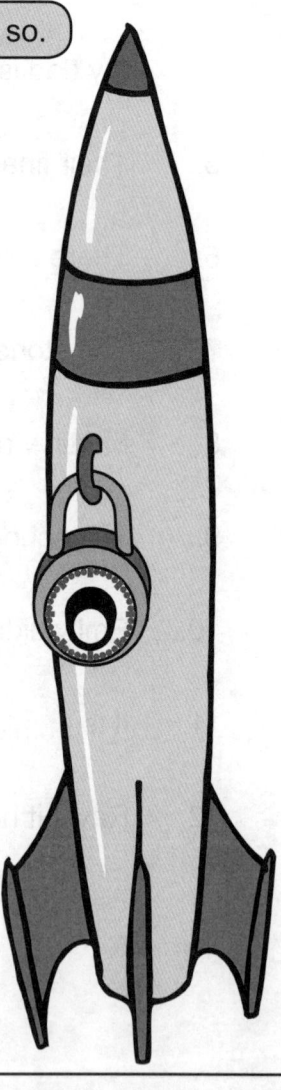

End of Set B: Scoresheet

You've finished a full set of tests — well done!

Now it's time to put your scores in here
and see how you're getting on.

	Score	
Test 1		/12
Test 2		/12
Test 3		/12
Test 4		/12
Spelling Test		/12
Total		**/60**

Once you've got a score out of 60, check it out in the table below...

0 – 29	If you got a lot of questions wrong, don't worry. Ask an adult to help you work out the **areas** you need **more practice** on. Then have another go at **this** set of tests.
30 – 45	If you got half-marks or better, you're doing well. **Read** back over your **incorrect** answers and make sure you know **why** they're wrong. Then try the **next set** of tests.
46 – 60	Woohoo! Now have a go at the **next set** of tests — can you beat your score?

Set C: Grammar & Punctuation 1

There are **12 questions** in this test. Give yourself **10 minutes** to answer them all.

1. Circle the words that should start with a **capital letter** in the sentence below.

   the tigers were seen leaving the zoo last tuesday.

   1 mark

2. Put a tick in each row to show whether each underlined word in the sentence below is an **adjective** or an **adverb**.

   We gasped <u>loudly</u> when the <u>famous</u> magician <u>suddenly</u> appeared.

Word	Adjective	Adverb
loudly		
famous		
suddenly		

   Adjectives describe nouns, but adverbs often describe verbs.

   1 mark

3. Put a prefix at the start of each word below to make it mean the **opposite**.

   ....agree

   ....kind

   1 mark

4. Put a tick in each row to show whether each sentence is an **exclamation** or a **command**.

Sentence	Exclamation	Command
What a fabulous trip that was		
Take the green bins out now		
Don't touch my slice of cake		

1 mark

5. Tick the sentence that uses **direct speech** correctly.

tick **one** box

Idir "said he thought plays were boring." ☐

Linda cried "go home now". ☐

"What's the matter?" I asked. ☐

"There's a kite festival today", said the man. ☐

1 mark

6. Underline the **relative pronoun** in each of the sentences below.

The ruby, which we found in China, is very valuable.

Never trust a chef whose kitchen is dirty.

1 mark

7. Tick **one** box to show the **co-ordinating conjunction** in the sentence below.

> Co-ordinating conjunctions can be used to join two main clauses together.

I bought some pizza for dinner this evening, but Paula had already cooked spaghetti.

1 mark

8. Tick the **two** sentences that use a **dash** correctly.

tick **two** boxes

I couldn't see — it was too dark. ☐

They — went home to the farm. ☐

There is a large volcano on — the island. ☐

Josh hid from the lion — he was scared of it. ☐

1 mark

9. Underline the **subordinate clause** in each of the sentences below.

We walked the dog because it needed some exercise.

Before I took lessons, I couldn't paint very well.

1 mark

10. The sentence below is missing a **semi-colon**.
    Tick **one** box to show where the semi-colon should go.

    My bike was very dirty I decided to wash it.

    1 mark

11. Draw a line to show whether each sentence is written in the **active** voice or the **passive** voice. The first one has been done for you.

    Dave slept on the comfy sofa. ——— active

    The sun was covered by the clouds.

    We trained together for the marathon. passive

    1 mark

12. Read the sentence below.
    Write the **present progressive** form of the underlined verb in the box.

    The present progressive form shows something that's happening right now.

    Sally's sister <u>drives</u> to the airport.

    1 mark

END OF TEST

/12

Set C: Grammar & Punctuation 2

There are **12 questions** in this test. Give yourself **10 minutes** to answer them all.

1. Add **two full stops** to the sentences below so that they are punctuated correctly.

   Last year, I was in America California was incredible

   1 mark

2. The sentences in the table are missing either '**a**' or '**an**'.
   Put a tick in the right column for each one.

Sentence	a	an
My soup had ... fly in it.		
We took Raheem to see ... exciting film.		
Learning French was ... difficult challenge.		

   1 mark

3. Underline the **preposition** in the sentence below.

   Jasmine found some purple flowers under the trees.

   1 mark

4. Put a letter in each box to show which **word class** the underlined words belong to.

| pronoun A | conjunction B | noun C |

The <u>swimmer</u> hurt her arm, <u>so</u> the lifeguard helped <u>her</u>.

1 mark

5. Rewrite the question below as a **statement**.

Can you buy train tickets at the ticket office?

A statement is a sentence that tells you something.

....

....

1 mark

6. Draw a line to match each word to the correct **suffix**. The first one has been done for you.

test —— ify
final   ful
fox   ise
taste   es

Only use each suffix once.

1 mark

Set C: Grammar & Punctuation 2

7. Tick the sentence that uses a **comma** correctly.

tick **one** box

After the talent show, let's get some ice cream. ☐

Japan, where I used to live is in Asia. ☐

During, the film my sister fell asleep. ☐

1 mark

8. Add one **bracket** to each sentence below so that they are punctuated correctly.

The sentences should still make sense without the words inside the brackets.

That picture the black and white one) is really old.

Her sister (my best friend is turning ten tomorrow.

1 mark

9. Read the information in the box below.
Write **one sentence** that lists all this information.
Make sure you use correct punctuation in your answer.

Flavours of milkshake
banana
chocolate
strawberry

....

....

....

1 mark

Set C: Grammar & Punctuation 2

10. Underline the **relative clause** in the sentence below.

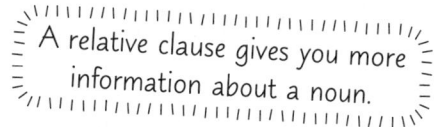
A relative clause gives you more information about a noun.

Our brother, who is older than us, is moving to Newcastle.

1 mark

11. Underline the **adverbial** in the sentence below.

After school, I practised my gymnastics routine.

1 mark

12. Tick **one** box to show the **modal verb** in the sentence below.

We could go to visit Will tomorrow.

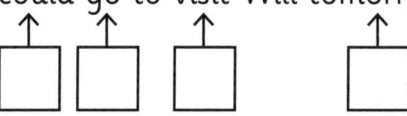

1 mark

END OF TEST

/12

Set C: Grammar & Punctuation 3

There are **11 questions** in this test. Give yourself **10 minutes** to answer them all.

1. Tick the **two** sentences that are **questions**.

   tick **two** boxes

   Why is your hair so messy ☐

   What a spooky story that was ☐

   Would you like to buy this coat ☐

   How nice it was to bump into you ☐

   1 mark

2. Underline the longest **noun phrase** in the sentence below.

   A noisy pink helicopter flew over our house.

   1 mark

3. Read the sentences below. Tick the **two** sentences that use the **simple present** tense.

   tick **two** boxes

   We took the long way home. ☐

   Mike plays squash on Thursdays. ☐

   The whole family knits together. ☐

   The superhero is going to save the day. ☐

   1 mark

4. Read the sentences below. Circle the **pronoun** in brackets which completes each sentence.

Those football boots are (her / hers / she).

I remember when (us / we / our) went to the seaside.

1 mark

5. The sentence below is missing a **comma**.
Tick **one** box to show where the comma should go.

Despite leaving ↑ early ↑ Gopal ↑ still managed to arrive ↑ late.
☐ ☐ ☐ ☐

1 mark

6. Each of the sentences below is missing a **verb**.
Draw a line to match each sentence with the correct verb.

My dad is .... with my mum.	danced
Yesterday, they .... for four hours.	dance
We .... when the music comes on.	dancing

1 mark

7. Each sentence below is missing an **apostrophe**.
   Add in the apostrophes in the correct places.

   Sarah's car is in the garage.

   The men's shirts were stolen.

   The wolves' den was warm and cosy.

   1 mark

8. Underline the **subordinating conjunction** in the sentence below.

   Rochelle will look after Satoshi's cats <u>until</u> he gets back.

   1 mark

9. Put a tick in the correct column to show whether the **subject** or the **object** is underlined. The first one has been done for you.

Sentence	Subject	Object
I picked up <u>the seashell</u>.		✓
<u>The pilot</u> landed the plane.		
Zara baked <u>an apple pie</u>.		

   In active sentences, the subject does something and the object has something done to it.

   1 mark

10. The sentence below is missing a **hyphen**.
    Tick **one** box to show where the hyphen should go.

    There are twenty one seats on this red bus.

    1 mark

11. Complete the table below by writing a suitable **synonym** or **antonym** in each empty box. Some have been done for you.

Word	Synonym	Antonym
funny	humorous	serious
hungry		
enormous		

2 marks

END OF TEST

/12

Set C: Grammar & Punctuation 4

There are **12 questions** in this test. Give yourself **10 minutes** to answer them all.

1. Underline the **adjective** in the sentence below.

   If it's a clear night, Jonny will go and look at the stars.

   1 mark

2. Look at the table below. Put a tick in each row to show which **punctuation mark** should be used at the end of each sentence.

Sentence	Exclamation mark	Question mark
How do I do this		
How stupid it was to try that		
How will we get home now		

   1 mark

3. Read the sentences below. Circle the word in brackets which completes each sentence in **Standard English**.

   We were with (those / them) children all day.

   Sandip and (I / me) reached the top of the hill.

   1 mark

4. Circle the **determiner** in each sentence below.

    Lesedi found the missing diamond today.

    Sabrina decided to have some pasta.

    1 mark

5. Rewrite the sentence below so that Carina's words are in **direct speech**.

    Inverted commas go around what is being said.

    Tomorrow, we should go swimming, said Carina.

    ....

    ....

    1 mark

6. Read the sentence below.
    Circle the correct option to complete the sentence so that it uses the **present perfect** form.

    The present perfect is used to talk about things that have already happened.

    My sister .... rugby here.

    plays   has played   will play   is playing

    1 mark

7. Add a **colon** to the sentence below so that it's punctuated correctly.

A colon can introduce a list.

We gave lots of things to charity some shirts , my old toy car and a few books.

1 mark

8. Tick the **two** sentences that use **adverbials**.

tick **two** boxes

The runner finished the race quite slowly. ☐

Craig put his shoes on and crept outside. ☐

Later on, the class will have a visitor. ☐

Our brown dog likes to take long naps. ☐

1 mark

9. Tick the sentence that uses **semi-colons** correctly.

tick **one** box

I need plenty of screws (to hold it up); some tools, which I'll borrow from Joe; and a really tall ladder. ☐

The fossil; which was really old; was in good condition. ☐

Liam enjoys; golf, basketball and computer games. ☐

1 mark

10. Read the sentence below.
    Using the verb in brackets, complete the sentence in the **present progressive** form.

    We .... a film.   (to watch)

    1 mark

11. Tick the sentence which is written in the **passive** voice.

	tick **one** box
Michelle went to the shops.	☐
The wall was hit by the lorry.	☐
The frog leapt across the pond.	☐
We built a new cabinet.	☐

    1 mark

12. Look at the **word family** below.
    What does the root <u>aud</u> mean?

    | audio | | audience | | audible |

	tick **one** box
crowd	☐
hear	☐
enjoy	☐

    1 mark

END OF TEST

/12

Set C: Spelling Test

For this test, you'll need someone to **read out** the transcript from the middle of the book, or you can use the **online audio file**. The test will take about 10 minutes.

mark box

1. A .... of girls entered the post office.

2. We wanted to .... a treehouse.

3. The .... was wet after the rain.

4. The artist had .... finished their painting.

5. Clara took a .... of the woman in the hat.

6. The .... to the shop was blocked.

7. Romina .... Carey a new umbrella.

8. The teacher's expression was very ....

9. It has been an .... day out.

10. The players were polite to the ....

11. I burnt my .... on my hot chocolate.

12. The .... did all of his homework on time.

/12

Set C: Puzzle

This puzzle is a brilliant way to practise your spelling skills.

Royal Riddle

Queen Felicity is preparing for a big feast. While everyone is getting ready, an old wizard appears and threatens to curse the castle unless someone can solve his riddle. Each of the sentences below contains a misspelt word. Find the letter that is missing from each misspelt word and write it in the box. Once you have found all six missing letters, unscramble them to answer the wizard's riddle.

1. The gardener is sweeping autum leaves off the paths.

2. The king is artisticlly decorating the hall.

3. The princess is looking for a pair of sissors.

4. The cook is making a batch of lemonad.

5. The hansome prince is brushing his hair.

6. The queen is franticaly trying to solve the riddle.

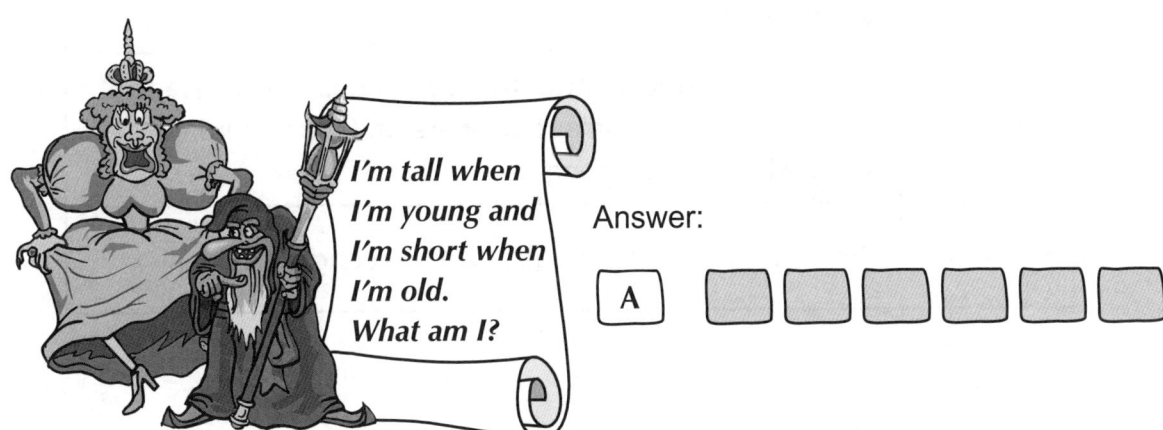

I'm tall when I'm young and I'm short when I'm old. What am I?

Answer: A ☐ ☐ ☐ ☐ ☐ ☐

End of Set C: Scoresheet

You've finished a full set of tests — well done!

Now it's time to put your scores in here
and see how you're getting on.

	Score	
Test 1		/12
Test 2		/12
Test 3		/12
Test 4		/12
Spelling Test		/12
Total		**/60**

Once you've got a score out of 60, check it out in the table below...

0 – 29	If you got a lot of questions wrong, don't worry. Ask an adult to help you work out the **areas** you need **more practice** on. Then have another go at **this** set of tests.
30 – 45	If you got half-marks or better, you're doing well. **Read** back over your **incorrect** answers and make sure you know **why** they're wrong.
46 – 60	Woohoo! You've done really well — congratulations!

Hints and Tips

*Grammar, punctuation and spelling can be a bit tricky.
If you get stuck, this page might help you out.*

1. **Learn** the **main parts** of speech.

    The <u>children</u> <u>baked</u> some <u>delicious</u> biscuits.

    Noun　　　　**Verb**　　　　**Adjective**
    (a naming word)　(a doing or　　(a describing word)
    　　　　　　　　being word)

2. Make sure you can identify the different **parts** of a **sentence.**

    <u>The runner decided to slow down</u> <u>because her legs were tired</u>.

    Main Clause　　　　　　**Subordinate Clause**
    (the most important clause)　(the less important clause)

3. Always use **capital letters** for proper nouns and after **full stops, exclamation marks** and **question marks.**

    Proper noun

    It's pouring with rain. What a horrible day it is! Has Ben got his umbrella?

    Capital letter　**Full stop**　**Exclamation mark**　**Question mark**

4. **Apostrophes** show **missing letters**, or that something **belongs** to someone.

    I'll see you tomorrow.　　　　　Lucy's apple
    (This is a **contracted form** of 'I will'.)　(This is to show **possession**.)

5. **Break** words down into **smaller parts** to help you spell them.
    e.g.　par-tic-u-lar　　in-div-id-u-al　　com-pe-ti-tion

Answers

Set A

Test 1 – Pages 2-5

1. What a tremendous show that was (**1 mark**)

2. We saw a bridge ↑ a skyscraper ↑✓ and ↑ a stadium. (**1 mark**)

3. Michael danced in the <u>local</u> competition. I'm <u>furious</u> that Billy barely tried to help us. (**1 mark for both correct**)

4. I put up the tent <u>while</u> Anika collected wood. (**1 mark**)

5. Natalie said the green bike was <u>hers</u>. The paint is <u>ours</u> because we paid for it. I thought the magazine was <u>mine</u>. (**1 mark for all correct**)

6. dread — ful
   move — ness
   fault — less
   ill — ment

   (dread–ful, move–ment, fault–less, ill–ness)
   (**1 mark for all correct**)

7. Sarah put the cake tin on the table. (**1 mark**)

8. They went into the cave, <u>where it was very gloomy</u>. (**1 mark**)

9. Louise <u>has written</u> a short story. (**1 mark**)

10. The museum was boring; I went to the cinema. (**1 mark**)

11. Gina is closing the curtains. (**1 mark**)

12. Answers may vary, for example:
    He said, "The shop is closed." (**1 mark**)

Test 2 – Pages 6-9

1. They asked me to visit, but i can't go ↑ ↑✓
   to germany this year. ↑✓ ↑
   (**1 mark for both correct**)

2.
Sentence	Full stop	Question mark
Tamara will be back soon	✓	
When does the plane arrive		✓
This isn't Kyle's house	✓	

(**1 mark for all correct**)

3. I drew on <u>the shiny whiteboard</u> yesterday. (**1 mark**)

4. The skater skidded around the corner. Giselle trekked up the tallest mountain. (**1 mark for both correct**)

5.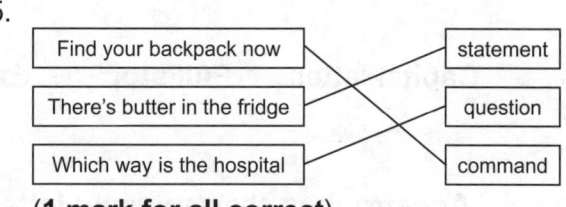

(Find your backpack now – command; There's butter in the fridge – statement; Which way is the hospital – question)
(**1 mark for all correct**)

6. he
   they
   (**1 mark for both correct**)

Answers   60

Answers

7. The twins rode their bikes to Sams house to see his new gerbils.
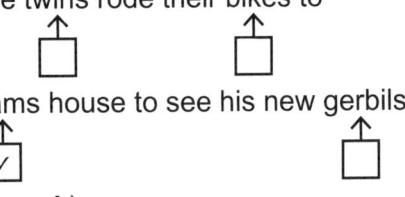
(**1 mark**)

8. <u>The customers</u> ate <u>the soup</u>.
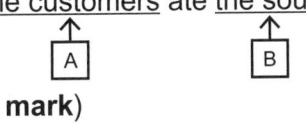
(**1 mark**)

9.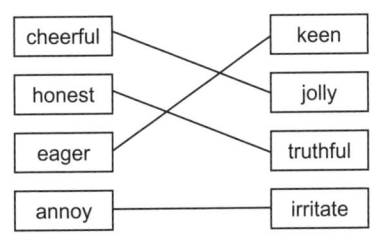
cheerful — jolly
honest — truthful
eager — keen
annoy — irritate
(**1 mark for all correct**)

10. I really like cats — I draw pictures of them all the time. (**1 mark**)

11. Answers may vary, for example:
Verb — We wash the car on Saturdays.
Noun — I had a wash this morning.
(**1 mark for one correct, 2 marks for both correct**)

Test 3 – Pages 10-13

1. The talented <u>teenager</u> played his <u>flute</u> perfectly.
(**1 mark for both correct**)

2. Tomorrow evening, I am going to my piano lesson. (**1 mark**)

3. We saw some monkeys and a zebra. (**1 mark**)

4. The goldfish my first pet is a year old today.
(**1 mark for both correct**)

5. Nisha thought it would be sunny, <u>so</u> she brought a hat <u>and</u> a bottle of water. However, she didn't bring her sunglasses <u>or</u> a picnic for lunch.
(**1 mark for all correct**)

6.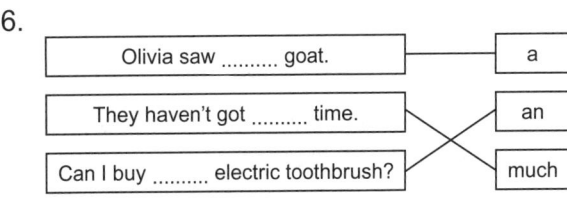
Olivia saw .... goat. — a
They haven't got .... time. — much
Can I buy .... electric toothbrush? — an
(**1 mark for all correct**)

7.

Adjective	Adverb
quick	quickly
furious	**furiously**
sloppy	**sloppily**

(**1 mark for both correct**)

8. It <u>might</u> snow later today. (**1 mark**)

9. The pet-friendly hotel was excellent. (**1 mark**)

10. I met a girl <u>who</u> was from Australia. Let's find a clover <u>that</u> has four leaves. The chicken, <u>which</u> lives in the barn, is very noisy.
(**1 mark for all correct**)

Answers

11. Akira is going to do these things:
    - finish his history homework
    - play baseball
    - read a book

    Answers with commas or semi-colons after each of the first two items and a full stop after the third are also acceptable. The use of a capital letter at the start of every item is also acceptable.
    (**1 mark for any correct answer with consistent punctuation and capitalisation**)

12. foot (**1 mark**)

Test 4 – Pages 14-17

1. The guards <u>wouldnt</u> let the reporters into the bank. (**1 mark**)

2.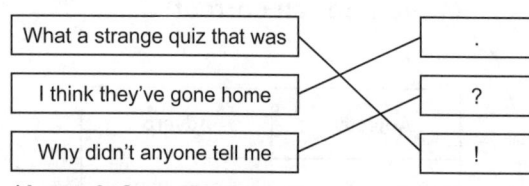
   (**1 mark for all correct**)

3. My baby sister cried <u>because</u> she was hungry.
   Tyler always grumbles <u>when</u> he cleans his room.
   (**1 mark for both correct**)

4. a main clause (**1 mark**)

5. Get down before they see you. (**1 mark**)

6. The fairground ride was over <u>very quickly</u>. (**1 mark**)

7.
Sentence	Formal	Informal
The house is freezing, don't you think?		✓
We are delighted to accept this award.	✓	
It is vital that he attend.	✓	

(**1 mark for all correct**)

8.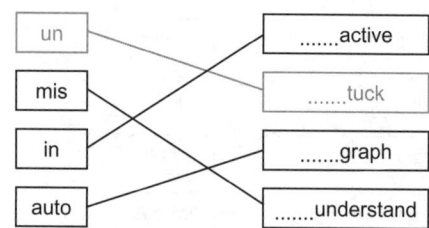
   (**1 mark for all correct**)

9. We were happy: Dad said we could go to the park. (**1 mark**)

10. Grace, who is good at art, will draw a picture. (**1 mark**)

11. Answers may vary, for example:
    The first sentence means that Harry buys chocolate cake, but the second sentence means that Harry buys chocolate and cake. (**1 mark**)

12. The bulldozer destroyed the mansion. (**1 mark**)

Answers

Spelling Test – Page 18

1. happily (**1 mark**)
2. quite (**1 mark**)
3. station (**1 mark**)
4. research (**1 mark**)
5. trouble (**1 mark**)
6. special (**1 mark**)
7. echo (**1 mark**)
8. arrive (**1 mark**)
9. sensible (**1 mark**)
10. flies (**1 mark**)
11. travel (**1 mark**)
12. mystery (**1 mark**)

Puzzle – Page 19

The words are: newly, slyly, moody, dirty, jogging, stopping, losses and cities.

Set B

Test 1 – Pages 21-24

1. The kangaroo <u>bounced</u> towards the meadow. (**1 mark**)
2. Ellen <u>rows</u> her boat down the river. (**1 mark**)
3. Abha's pebble was smoother than mine
   I might do my homework on the bus
   (**1 mark for both correct**)
4. I left my wallet at home, <u>so</u> Abbey paid for dinner. (**1 mark**)
5. Early each morning Pascal goes for a jog. (tick on second box) (**1 mark**)
6. a noun phrase (**1 mark**)
7. The shop sells these items:
   - camping equipment
   - hiking boots
   - sunglasses

   Answers with commas or semi-colons after each of the first two items and a full stop after the third are also acceptable. The use of a capital letter at the start of every item is also acceptable.
   (**1 mark for any correct answer with consistent punctuation and capitalisation**)
8. My <u>brave</u> sister <u>fearlessly</u> took <u>the</u> spider outside.
   (brave = A, fearlessly = C, the = B)
   (**1 mark for all correct**)
9. I dislike three things: moths, wasps and bees.
   Hachiro was upset: he'd lost his backpack.
   (**1 mark for both correct**)
10. My ball — which I got on holiday — is stuck in a tree.
    (**1 mark for both correct**)
11. Answers may vary, for example:

Word	Antonym
wet	dry
sleepy	alert
boring	exciting

    (**1 mark for both correct**)
12. If I were a bear, I would eat nothing but honey. (**1 mark**)

Answers

Test 2 – Pages 25-28

1. saturday (**1 mark**)

2. She found a rare coin and hid it in the wardrobe.
   (ticks above "She" and "hid")
   (**1 mark for both correct**)

3. Answers may vary, for example:
   Take Ryan to his doctor's appointment.
   (**1 mark**)

4. super- (**1 mark**)

5. ours (**1 mark**)

6. Do you think we should leave, Leigh?
   (**1 mark**)

7. The cat was sitting outside. (**1 mark**)

8. Sophie made her way slowly through the tunnel. (**1 mark**)

9. On my pizza, I normally have tomatoes, but not too many; a few mushrooms; and plenty of cheese.
   (**1 mark for both correct**)

10. Claude won the trophy <u>because he beat Florence</u>. (**1 mark**)

11. A well known author visited our school last week.
    (tick above "well")
    (**1 mark**)

12.

Sentence	Passive	Active
The swan landed in the pond.		✓
Ben sings into the microphone.		✓
The lamp was knocked over by the child.	✓	

(**1 mark for both correct**)

Test 3 – Pages 29-32

1. noun (**1 mark**)

2. The zoo had giant pandas, zebras and elephants. (**1 mark**)

3. Mrs Harrison is coming over later, said Joey.
   (ticks above "Mrs" and below after "over" and "said")
   (**1 mark for both correct**)

4. We <u>aren't</u> doing our homework tonight.
   I don't want <u>anything</u> on my toast.
   (**1 mark for both correct**)

5. ran
   passed
   (**1 mark for both correct**)

6. She has lived in Canada for years.
   (**1 mark**)

7. John, <u>whose</u> birthday it was, missed his own party. (**1 mark**)

8. On Sundays, Nadeema goes for long bike rides. (**1 mark**)

Answers

9.

Sentence	Main clause	Subordinate clause
Jess uses Bruce's room when he is away.	✓	
After the river flooded, the road was closed.		✓
I cleaned my boots before I came inside.		✓

(**1 mark for all correct**)

10. I ate fried squid for the first time it was delicious. (**1 mark**) [tick in third box]

11. The parrot held <u>the cracker</u>.
    Answers that only underline 'cracker' are also acceptable. (**1 mark**)

12. squeeze (**1 mark**)

Test 4 – Pages 33-36

1. exclamation (**1 mark**)

2. Marlene listens to pop music all the time, <u>but</u> she never listens to country music. (**1 mark**)

3. How disgusting that was!
   How did the thief get into the safe?
   (**1 mark for both correct**)

4. We discovered that the statue was <u>theirs</u>.
   I forgot to bring a coat, so Gareth lent me <u>his</u>.
   (**1 mark for both correct**)

5. Answers may vary, for example:
   When did you arrive at the campsite?
   (**1 mark**)

6. a main clause (**1 mark**)

7. You'll need these things for school a jumper, a bag, a pencil case and a new set of pens. (**1 mark**) [tick in second box and fourth box]

8. She will <u>probably</u> meet us at the supermarket. (**1 mark**)

9. hopeless (**1 mark**)

10. We hid in the cupboard, <u>which was very cramped</u>. (**1 mark**)

11. We should invite our friends over at the weekend. (**1 mark**) [tick in first box]

12. Answers may vary, for example:
    The first sentence means the shoes belong to one girl, but the second sentence means the shoes belong to more than one girl. (**1 mark**)

Spelling Test – Page 37

1. paper (**1 mark**)
2. worth (**1 mark**)
3. young (**1 mark**)
4. nicest (**1 mark**)
5. science (**1 mark**)
6. eight (**1 mark**)
7. rough (**1 mark**)
8. position (**1 mark**)
9. gardener (**1 mark**)
10. notice (**1 mark**)
11. illegal (**1 mark**)
12. ceiling (**1 mark**)

Answers

Puzzle – Page 38

You should have underlined:

Ms Wright's Year <u>Eight</u> class was the biggest in the school.

That's the last time I'm telling you <u>three</u> anything!

James's uncle gave him a <u>five</u> pound note.

I called Zuri's number <u>six</u> times, but she didn't answer.

We're going to sing <u>four</u> songs at Erika's wedding.

The code to unlock the spaceship is: 83564

Set C

Test 1 – Pages 40-43

1. <u>the</u> tigers were seen leaving the zoo last <u>tuesday</u>.
   (**1 mark for both correct**)

2.
Word	Adjective	Adverb
loudly		✓
famous	✓	
suddenly		✓

   (**1 mark for all correct**)

3. disagree
   unkind
   (**1 mark for both correct**)

4.
Sentence	Exclamation	Command
What a fabulous trip that was	✓	
Take the green bins out now		✓
Don't touch my slice of cake		✓

   (**1 mark for all correct**)

5. "What's the matter?" I asked. (**1 mark**)

6. The ruby, <u>which</u> we found in China, is very valuable.
   Never trust a chef <u>whose</u> kitchen is dirty.
   (**1 mark for both correct**)

7. I bought some pizza for dinner this evening, but Paula had already cooked spaghetti. (The ✓ arrow points to between "had" and "already".) (**1 mark**)

8. I couldn't see — it was too dark.
   Josh hid from the lion — he was scared of it.
   (**1 mark for both correct**)

9. We walked the dog <u>because it needed some exercise</u>.
   <u>Before I took lessons</u>, I couldn't paint very well.
   (**1 mark for both correct**)

10. My bike was very dirty I decided to wash it. (The ✓ arrow points between "dirty" and "I".) (**1 mark**)

Answers   66

Answers

11.

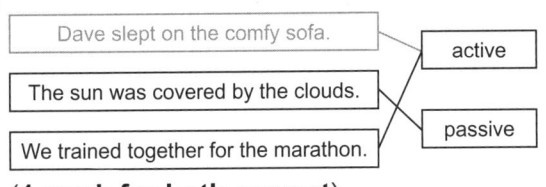

(**1 mark for both correct**)

12. is driving (**1 mark**)

Test 2 – Pages 44-47

1. Last year, I was in America. California was incredible.
(**1 mark for both correct**)

2.

Sentence	a	an
My soup had ... fly in it.		✓
We took Raheem to see ... exciting film.		✓
Learning French was ... difficult challenge.	✓	

(**1 mark for all correct**)

3. Jasmine found some purple flowers <u>under</u> the trees. (**1 mark**)

4. The <u>swimmer</u> hurt her arm, <u>so</u> the
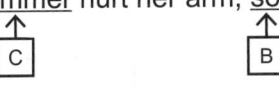
lifeguard helped <u>her</u>.

(**1 mark for all correct**)

5. Answers may vary, for example:
You can buy train tickets at the ticket office. (**1 mark**)

6.

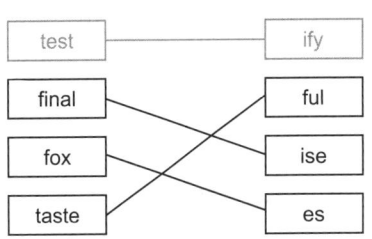

(**1 mark for all correct**)

7. After the talent show, let's get some ice cream. (**1 mark**)

8. That picture (the black and white one) is really old.
Her sister (my best friend) is turning ten tomorrow.
(**1 mark for both correct**)

9. Answers may vary, for example:
The flavours of milkshake are banana, chocolate and strawberry.
(**1 mark for any correctly punctuated sentence that lists all of the information**)

10. Our brother, <u>who is older than us</u>, is moving to Newcastle. (**1 mark**)

11. <u>After school</u>, I practised my gymnastics routine. (**1 mark**)

12. We could go to visit Will tomorrow.
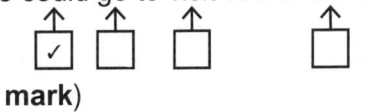
(**1 mark**)

Test 3 – Pages 48-51

1. Why is your hair so messy
Would you like to buy this coat
(**1 mark for both correct**)

2. <u>A noisy pink helicopter</u> flew over our house. (**1 mark**)

Answers

3. Mike plays squash on Thursdays.
   The whole family knits together.
   (**1 mark for both correct**)

4. Those football boots are <u>hers</u>.
   I remember when <u>we</u> went to the seaside.
   (**1 mark for both correct**)

5. Despite leaving early Gopal still managed to arrive late.
   (arrow marked on second box ✓; arrow pointing up below "to arrive late")
   (**1 mark**)

6. My dad is .... with my mum. — dancing
   Yesterday, they .... for four hours. — danced
   We .... when the music comes on. — dance
   (**1 mark for all correct**)

7. Sarah's car is in the garage.
   The men's shirts were stolen.
   The wolves' den was warm and cosy.
   (**1 mark for all correct**)

8. Rochelle will look after Satoshi's cats <u>until</u> he gets back. (**1 mark**)

9.
Sentence	Subject	Object
I picked up <u>the seashell</u>.		✓
<u>The pilot</u> landed the plane.	✓	
Zara baked <u>an apple pie</u>.		✓

(**1 mark for both correct**)

10. There are twenty one seats on this red bus.
    (arrows marked above "twenty" ✓ and "one"; arrow below "red")
    (**1 mark**)

11. Answers may vary, for example:

Word	Synonym	Antonym
funny	humorous	serious
hungry	starving	full
enormous	huge	tiny

(**1 mark for 2 correct, 2 marks for all correct**)

Test 4 – Pages 52-55

1. If it's a <u>clear</u> night, Jonny will go and look at the stars. (**1 mark**)

2.
Sentence	Exclamation mark	Question mark
How do I do this		✓
How stupid it was to try that	✓	
How will we get home now		✓

(**1 mark for all correct**)

3. We were with <u>those</u> children all day.
   Sandip and <u>I</u> reached the top of the hill.
   (**1 mark for both correct**)

Answers

Answers

4. Lesedi found <u>the</u> missing diamond today. Sabrina decided to have <u>some</u> pasta. (**1 mark for both correct**)

5. Answers may vary, for example: "Tomorrow, we should go swimming," said Carina. (**1 mark**)

6. has played (**1 mark**)

7. We gave lots of things to charity: some shirts, my old toy car and a few books. (**1 mark**)

8. The runner finished the race quite slowly. Later on, the class will have a visitor. (**1 mark for both correct**)

9. I need plenty of screws (to hold it up); some tools, which I'll borrow from Joe; and a really tall ladder. (**1 mark**)

10. We <u>are watching</u> a film. (**1 mark**)

11. The wall was hit by the lorry. (**1 mark**)

12. hear (**1 mark**)

Spelling Test – Page 56

1. group (**1 mark**)
2. build (**1 mark**)
3. earth (**1 mark**)
4. finally (**1 mark**)
5. picture (**1 mark**)
6. entrance (**1 mark**)
7. bought (**1 mark**)
8. serious (**1 mark**)
9. enjoyable (**1 mark**)
10. referee (**1 mark**)
11. tongue (**1 mark**)
12. student (**1 mark**)

Puzzle – Page 57

1. The gardener is sweeping autum<u>n</u> leaves off the paths.
2. The king is artistic<u>all</u>y decorating the hall.
3. The princess is looking for a pair of s<u>c</u>issors.
4. The cook is making a batch of lemonad<u>e</u>.
5. The han<u>d</u>some prince is brushing his hair.
6. The queen is frantical<u>l</u>y trying to solve the riddle.

Answer: A candle

Progress Chart

You've finished all the tests in the book — well done!

Now it's time to put your scores in here and see how you've done.

	Set A	Set B	Set C
Test 1			
Test 2			
Test 3			
Test 4			
Spelling Test			
Total			

See if you're on target by checking your marks for each set in the table below.

Mark	
0-29	You're not quite there yet, but don't worry — keep going back over the questions you find tricky and you'll improve your grammar, punctuation and spelling skills in no time.
30-45	You're getting there — good effort! Keep working on the topics you struggle with until you're really happy with them.
46-60	Give yourself a huge pat on the back — you've mastered this Foundation book! If you're ready to try something as hard as the real SATs, have a look at our Book 1 and Book 2 10-Minute Tests.